THE HIST(
LECKHAMPTON CHURCH
and its Parish

St Peter's Church
from a lithograph by George Rowe, *c*. 1840

THE HISTORY

of

LECKHAMPTON CHURCH

and its Parish

Eric Miller

St Peter's
Leckhampton Parish Church

Published by
St Peter's Parochial Church Council, Leckhampton,
The Rectory, Church Road, Leckhampton, GL53 0QJ
www.stpeters-leckhampton.org.uk

First edition 1987
Reprinted 1989
Revised edition 2006

ISBN 0-9512008-1-X

Typesetting and layout by the author

Printed by CGI Digital, 5 St Andrews Way, London E3 3PA

CONTENTS

INTRODUCTION AND ACKNOWLEDGEMENTS

Twenty years have elapsed since the first edition of this book was prepared, and the need for a reprint has presented the opportunity of making revisions and additions. These are partly the result of continuing research but also of fresh material that has come to light, in particular some 'missing' Vestry minute books covering the years 1869-1940. As a result, the book has been extensively rewritten.

The village of Leckhampton lies below the Cotswold escarpment, where prehistoric remains have been found, and it is the location of one of the several moated sites dotted along the Severn Vale. The modern settlement, with its Saxon name, has its origins in the late eighth century. One of its manors listed in the Domesday Survey was for six centuries held by members of but three interrelated families. The manor house survives, now enjoying a renaissance as a Sue Ryder hospice, having served as a hospital in the First World War and a prisoner-of-war camp in the second, and later housing a private school. The village's medieval layout is hinted at by a few remaining thatched and timbered cottages. Its crowning glory, however, is its 14th-century church, whose slender spire is a conspicuous landmark in local stone. Small wonder that it is listed grade II* by English Heritage.

Leckhampton has deservedly attracted the attention of past historians. The parochial setting and the architectural features and monuments of the church have been described and illustrated in the standard histories of the county (by Sir Robert Atkyns in 1712 and Samuel Rudder in 1779), by David Verey and Alan Brookes in Pevsner's *Buildings of England* series, and in articles in such journals as the *Transactions of the Bristol and Gloucester Archaeological Society*. Short descriptive booklets were written by Leonard Barnard in 1931 and Alfred Bendall in 1956, and a chapter is devoted to the church in Eve Andrew and Eric Brewin's *Leckhampton through the*

Ages (1979), while Robert Cary Barnard's *Records of Leckhampton*, published in 1897, recounts the earlier history of the parish.

Inspired by such predecessors, this book aims to distil the numerous references to the building and ecclesiastical parish found in all the available sources, published and unpublished, and present them in their historical context. However, much more could be added about the stained glass and the memorials inside the church and about the notable people buried in the churchyard, and these subjects will in due course be covered in another book.

Most of the illustrations are new to this edition. As well as photographs, they include some drawings and engravings showing the church as it appeared in the 18th and 19th centuries. Where no acknowledgement is given, the illustrations are either my own or are taken from the archives of the Local History Society or St Peter's.

For access to original documents, I thank the appropriate authorities at the Gloucestershire Archives, the Gloucester City Library and Cheltenham Public Library (Local History Collections). I am indebted to Canon George Smith, who originally asked me to undertake this project when he was Rector of Leckhampton and who thereby fostered my interest in Leckhampton's past, and to the Reverend Paul Wilkinson, the present incumbent, for his encouragement. I also thank expert friends who looked at the draft and made useful suggestions for its improvement, especially Michael Greet who offered guidance on sources and their interpretation when I first embarked on the task. Not least, I thank my wife, Margaret, for her patience during the book's long preparation and for her help in proof-reading.

Eric Miller
July 2006

HISTORIC BOUNDARY OF LECKHAMPTON PARISH

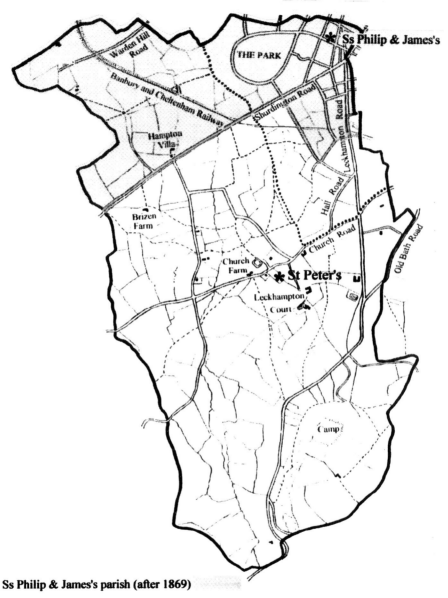

Ss Philip & James's parish (after 1869)

Cheltenham Borough boundary (after 1894) ••••••

Drawn by Bruce Stait 1994
Based on Ordnance Survey map 1888

1
PRIESTS, PEOPLE AND PATRONS

The Medieval Parish

Leckhampton's beginnings can be traced back to about 770 AD, by which time a home farm serving the royal manor at Cheltenham had been established there. No church or chapel was mentioned then or in the Domesday Survey of 1086, but it is likely that one had been built by 1133, when Henry I endowed the collegiate church at Cirencester with the church at Cheltenham and its attached chapels. One of these chapels was clearly at Leckhampton, for in about 1162 its priest, Henry, was summoned before Archbishop Thomas à Becket over a dispute with the Canons of the Abbey of Cirencester about the payment of dues. Leckhampton's relative importance may be judged from the fact that its dues were the very least payable to the abbey, a mere two shillings, while some churches paid 20 or even 50 shillings a year.

The chapel of Leckhampton continued to pay dues (still two shillings in 1303) to the Abbot and Convent of Cirencester Abbey until the dissolution of the monasteries in 1539. In the early twelfth century certain lands in the parish were owned by the Canons of Llantony Priory, who allowed the lord of the manor's chaplain to enjoy a portion of the tithes arising from them. In 1535 the Rector of Leckhampton was farming the same lands, rented from the prior's bailiff.

The patrons of the living were normally the lords of the manor. However, as will be seen later, the gift of patronage (or 'advowson') was a commodity that could be bought and sold or mortgaged to raise money. As an added complication, reflecting England's close links with France in the centuries following the Norman Conquest, the advowson was for a time possessed by the Abbot of Fécamp in Normandy, though in practice the duty of patron was carried out locally by members of the Despenser and Giffard families.

There is no record of a formal dedication of the church, but the accepted dedication to St Peter can be traced to at least the early 16th century. Roger Norwood's will of 1512 contains a reference to the high altar of Leckhampton church and St Peter, and this is confirmed by subsequent records. There was no justification for the usage, current locally in the 1960s, of 'St Peter and St Paul'. Equally, a survey of the diocese in 1735, which listed Leckhampton as 'St John', must have been an isolated aberration. (Not to mention Norman May's *Guide to Cheltenham* of 1890, which repeatedly refers to Leckhampton church as dedicated to St Mary!)

The names of some early priests of Leckhampton are included in the list at Appendix A on page 65, though the records are not complete until the late 16th century. Henry was still in his post in 1199. The earlier episode evidently had not harmed his career, as he was by then described as a rural dean. By 1270 the incumbent was a rector, implying that his church had been granted independence of that at Cheltenham; he would also have been entitled to the tithes from glebe land.

In 1327, at the time when the first enlargement of the church was taking place, there were at least 23 taxpaying residents of Leckhampton, though it is not known how many 'lower orders' were omitted.

The diocesan authority was the Bishop of Worcester until Gloucester diocese was formed in 1541. The earliest recorded Bishop's visitation of the parish took place on 10 March 1340, when the Bishop of Worcester was performing a tour of the deanery of Winchcombe, in which Leckhampton was then situated. The visitation took place in the church itself, after which the bishop moved on to Cheltenham, where he dined and spent the night.

Roger Norwood, lord of the manor who died in 1512, bequeathed 6s. 8d. (about 34 new pence) to the high altar of the church of Leckynton (Leckington – an alternative name for the village that was still in popular use until the 1930s). In addition, 12d. each was to be given towards supplying oil or candles for the rood light (i.e. one placed before a crucifix suspended in the chancel arch) and for a light dedicated to Our Lady. The rood light was remembered in another will in 1546, a bushel of wheat being left for its maintenance. Roger Norwood also gave timber for the building of a 'new church house', or parish hall, which would customarily have been located within the churchyard (see Chapter 6). The house was mentioned in 1712 by Sir Robert Atkyns as being claimed by the lord of the manor.

The Reformation and After

As a consequence of the events of the English Reformation, clergy were required to swear to renounce the Bishop of Rome and declare lawful obedience to the Bishop of Gloucester. The earliest record of such an oath being taken at Leckhampton was in 1549, on the institution of Rhys Jones.

Not all incumbents appear to have taken easily to this transfer of allegiance. In 1570 Ralph Gynes (also spelt Geynes, Ginnis, Jenis Jenes, Jeynes and even Haines), described as 'literate, a minor in age', was sworn and admitted to the living, but by the following year he appears to have been deprived of it, and Anthony Higgins was instituted.

Higgins in his turn seems to have been an uneasy member of the Church of England. When instituted in March 1572 he was required to make an autographed subscription to the 39 Articles, but the entry was later scored through. In May a consistory court revoked his letters of institution but by the following year he appeared to have come to terms with the Articles, for he subscribed to them on being made Vicar of Painswick, though he remained there less than 12 months. At that time, Leckhampton's church seemed to be in poor repair, for 'the 'windows lacked glazing in default of the parson', who was admonished and ordered to repair them. Ralph Gynes, whose earlier departure could conceivably have been connected with problems of conscience or perhaps simply with his youth, was back in the parish as parson in 1576. A report following an archbishop's visitation described him as 'a meetelie divine' who 'understandeth Latin'. He subsequently signed a number of burial certificates; his own burial was recorded in 1612.

During William Norwood's long tenure as lord of the manor (1561 - 1632) the patronage was temporarily in the hands of others. Among these were in 1570 John Slaughter and William Badger, High Steward of the Court at Cheltenham, and in 1571 William Rogers (probably of Dowdeswell). The reason may have been that William Norwood was a recusant, i.e. a Catholic, failing to attend services of the church as ordered by the Acts of Uniformity. This unorthodoxy cannot have harmed him, for he was a powerful public figure, as lord of the manor of Cheltenham and High Sheriff of Gloucestershire. He is portrayed on the brass memorial to his wife in the Lady Chapel, and there is also a portrait of him in Cheltenham Art Gallery.

Detail from a portrait of William Norwood by Cornelius Jansen, dated 1619

Cheltenham Art Gallery and Museums

In the mid-17th century the Leckhampton living must have been a relatively comfortable one. According to a contemporary survey the Rector in 1650, who was a 'preaching minister' (i.e. one who was licensed or entitled by virtue of his education to preach sermons rather than simply read passages from the Homilies) with 40 families in his care, had an annual income of £80. By comparison, the ministers at Cheltenham and Charlton Kings had stipends of only £40 each.

Leckhampton's 'Vicar of Bray'

Robert Jones was Rector for 53 years from 1654 and died aged 84, one of several priests of Leckhampton who remained in office for over half a century. As well as being Rural Dean of Winchcombe he also found time to serve as Schoolmaster of Cheltenham Grammar School from 1674 to 1689. His daughter was buried in the churchyard of St Mary's, Cheltenham. In the circumstances it is perhaps not surprising that during those years priests from other parishes witnessed the burials at Leckhampton, such as Ralph Weld of Cheltenham and William Wynn of Charlton Kings.

Robert Jones's long incumbency may have assured some degree of stability during Cromwell's rule and after: he was a true 'Vicar of Bray'! His predecessor Rowland Crosby, on the other hand, had had the rectory of Leckhampton sequestered from him, very likely on account of his contrary views. In 1647, according to the Proceedings of the Committee for Plundered Ministries, his wife Dorothy was apportioned 'the full clear fifth part of all the tithes, rents, glebe lands and Easter book of the said benefice (all taxes and charges first deducted)'.

On Robert Jones's death in 1707 the Norwood family's connection with the church became still closer and Thomas Norwood was inducted as Rector – a 'squarson', in fact. He was also lord of the manor, though the patronage was evidently owned by one Arthur Charlett, according to the record of his institution. A distinguished man of his day, Arthur Charlett was Master of University College, Oxford, and Royal Chaplain. His unexpected involvement with Leckhampton is explained by the fact that he was Robert Jones's nephew.

Parish Registers

The surviving registers of baptisms, marriages and burials go back no further than 1682, but transcripts at the Gloucestershire Archives show that entries began to be made in 1601. By law, anyone who died after 1678 had to be buried in a woollen shroud, as a means of supporting an important native industry. The practice was last mentioned at Leckhampton in 1740, though in 1755 Leckhampton's Rector, John Trye, acted as witness to a 'burial in woollen' at Coberley.

A comparative rarity among the registers for the period 1679 - 1734 were special collections in aid of charitable causes outside the parish, and sometimes abroad, known as 'briefs' and authorised by the Bishop or even the King. The beneficiaries were mostly churches that were in need of repair or had been affected by fire or natural disasters, but in some cases individuals, buildings or streets were named. In October 1666, there was a collection for 'the late sad fire within the City of London'. In 1715 a brief was ordered in aid of 'cowkeepers', whose livelihood would have been affected by cattle plague in the previous year. 'Distressed Protestants' abroad were also remembered, especially the Huguenots persecuted by Louis XIV. These received £2 4s. 8d., but in general the sums involved were no more than a few shillings. Perhaps the most curious cause was the relief of prisoners of the Barbary pirates in Algiers and Morocco in 1680. It may be more than coincidence that the then lord of the manor, Colonel Henry Norwood, had some years previously served as Lieutenant-Governor of Tangier.

Long-lived Incumbents

Leckhampton's longest serving incumbent was Edward Draper, Rector for 58 years from 1767 to 1825. Regularly from 1810 onwards until the year of his death he was given permission to be absent from his benefice on account of his 'great age and bodily infirmity' and also because he was a licensed stipendiary curate at Alderley (near Wotton-under-Edge), where he lived. Leckhampton church was duly served by a vicarious priest in the pluralist Draper's absence, nominated by him and paid a £60 stipend plus surplice fees.

Canon Charles Brandon Trye, a descendant of Thomas Norwood, was Rector for 53 years from 1830, as well as lord of the manor from 1841. (He is not to be confused with his father of the same name, who among other accomplishments was a distinguished surgeon and encouraged Dr. Edward Jenner in his vaccination work.) Quite apart from rebuilding parts of Leckhampton Court, Canon Trye was responsible for encouraging a number of significant improvements and alterations in the parish, notably the enlargement of the church in the 1830s and 1860s and the erection of the original village school (now the dining room) in Hall Road in 1841.

The Rectory, built c.1830 by the Revd Charles Brandon Trye. His son Reginald, who followed him as Rector in 1888, was born there.

Dowell Conning

The Rectory

Probably on becoming rector, Canon Trye also built the present rectory on the foundations of an older house whose entrance had been in the lane opposite the church, near the moat. An inventory of 1679 had listed a 'parsonage house with barn, stable and outhouse on the west side of the common highway ... a little orchard adjoining [and] a pigeon house'. A parsonage is also shown on Crow's map of the parish, made in 1746. Presumably he went to live in it when it was completed, for his son Reginald stated that he had been born there (in 1843 – see below, page 17). From 1847 to 1865 Canon Trye was permitted by the bishop to 'reside out of the glebe house, occupying a mansion of his own' i.e. he had lived in Leckhampton Court rather than the rectory, though he moved back there in 1867, possibly for financial reasons. For portraits of the Canon and Reginald Trye see Appendix F, pages 72-74.

The 'Regency Gothic' St Philip's church, built in 1840. It was replaced by a larger building dedicated to St Philip and St James, in 1882.

Engraving by G P Johnson, c. 1840

The Parish subdivided: St Philip and St James's

To accommodate the growing population of gentry in The Park area and of artisans at the Bath Road end of the parish, Charles Brandon Trye and his brother Henry Norwood Trye (then living at Brandon House) promoted the building of a mission church on the corner of Grafton Road and Gratton Road, which was consecrated on St Philip and St James's day, 1840. Joseph Edmond Riddle was its first priest-in-charge and on his death in 1859 he was succeeded by Lawrence John Harrison, until then a curate at St Peter's. In 1869 the church and the area it served became independent of St Peter's. In 1882 the original building was replaced by the present one, considerably larger, designed by John Middleton, to which the distinctive saddle-back tower was added in 1902.

Sequestration of the Living, 1886

The last of the Tryes to serve as rector was Reginald, younger son of Charles Brandon Trye, who succeeded on his father's death in 1884. Two years later, however, he had run up substantial debts, sharing his family's financial difficulties over the quarries, and was declared bankrupt. The legal consequence was that the living was sequestered by the bishop and eventually placed in the care of a succession of curates-in-charge, while Reginald Trye remained, technically, the incumbent.

Reginald Trye continued in active ministry at Leckhampton until 1895, when he went to live in straitened circumstances in Milford Haven. He summed up his association with Leckhampton in a poignant letter written from the rectory for the parish magazine of August 1895:

> 'In this house I was born, and at our old parish church I was baptised and confirmed, and there I preached my first sermon ... and last Sunday I preached my last sermon'.

His career thus mirrors the fortunes of the Trye family as a whole, forced to sell the Leckhampton Court estate in 1894. The sequestration was not lifted until 1929, the year after his death at the age of 86.

The 20th Century and after

In the 20th century, two Rectors of Leckhampton were later consecrated bishop: Augustine Hodson (1915-21) as Bishop of Tewkesbury, and Eric Cordingly (1941-54) as Bishop of Thetford. Though appointed to Leckhampton in 1941, Eric Cordingly was on active service and was unable to take up his post until after the war. He was for three years a prisoner-of-war in Japanese hands, and during his absence the parish was in the care of Percy Unwin, assisted later on by Canon Baiter.

A significant change in the status of the incumbent took place in 2003. The Reverend Paul Wilkinson was appointed in that year as priest-in-charge rather than as rector. The main difference is that a priest-in-charge is, in theory, redeployable by the bishop. This move reflects the changing circumstances of the church in the 21st century, when clergy numbers are declining and St Peter's will be expected to work more closely with neighbouring parishes.

THE PATRONAGE

The arbitrary nature of the patron's power was well illustrated when Thomas Commeline was appointed as Rector of Leckhampton in 1825. He was placed under an obligation to resign when requested to do so, which suggests that Henry Norwood Trye, as patron, was preparing the way for his younger brother Charles to succeed. Five years later, Thomas Commeline duly ceded the living to Charles Brandon Trye.

The Leckhampton advowson, or patronage, changed hands several times during the 19th century. It could be mortgaged or, until prohibited by the Benefices Act of 1898, sold in order to raise capital, while it was a source of income for whoever held it. In 1821 it was granted for two years to Edward Machin of Whitemead Park in the Forest of Dean, and in 1843 it was conveyed from a consortium of local gentlemen to Charles Brandon Trye and his heirs. In 1880 Charles Brandon Trye, revoking an earlier will, bequeathed it to his older son Henry in preference to Reginald. In 1887, after his father's death, Henry remortgaged it to the Alliance Economic Investment Company for £6000.

Mrs Augusta Nevile Wyatt and the Transfer of the Patronage to the Bishop of Gloucester

In 1906 the advowson, which by that time included the benefice of St Philip and St James's as well as St Peter's, was transferred to the Bishop of Gloucester by Order in Council. The events immediately leading up to this transfer are worth summarising. When the Leckhampton Court estate was broken up in 1894 the advowson was included among the assets to be sold. It was bought outright, for the sum of £2500, by Mrs Augusta Warren Nevile Wyatt. She was the widow of a former East India Company planter, George Nevile Wyatt, of Lake House in Thirlestaine Road, who had been buried in St Peter's churchyard three years previously.

Mrs Wyatt's connection with Leckhampton is at first sight puzzling, especially as she was a member of the congregation at St Luke's, Cheltenham, and her husband had been a churchwarden there. However, in 1884 their daughter Annie married the Reverend William Clifford Aston, who was a son of the Vicar of St Luke's. When the living at St Peter's fell vacant on Reginald Trye's departure in 1895 Mrs Wyatt, as the new patron, was in a position to arrange the appointment of her son-in-law as the first of the curates-in-charge. This act of nepotism was perhaps forgivable, as Clifford Aston brought much energy and good fellowship to the village. He is best remembered now for inspiring the building of the Parish Hall as a centre of its social life.

Augusta Nevile Wyatt died in 1905, leaving the advowson to her two sons and three daughters. In 1906 it was sold to a Monmouth solicitor acting on behalf of an 'anonymous client' who wished to present the patronage to the Bishop of Gloucester.

In 1906 the curate-in-charge was Canon Henry Proctor, Clifford Aston having died two years previously. A revealing postscript to this episode is to be found in Canon Proctor's obituary report in the *Gloucestershire Echo* of 26 February 1912. It states that when he first came to Leckhampton he was able to persuade some churchmen to buy the advowson and make it over as a gift to the Bishop. 'He could not bear the idea that the care of souls should be at the mercy of the highest bidder in the open market.' It appears therefore that the 'anonymous client' may have been Canon Proctor himself; he was clearly instrumental in effecting the transfer.

The church in 1793
From Samuel Lysons's *Collection of Gloucestershire Antiquities*

2
THE PARISH CHURCH

The general shape and appearance of the church as it is now are essentially a legacy of the 14th century. The original work, using the locally quarried limestone to good effect, remained unaltered until Victorian times, and much of it can still be recognised in the chancel, the porch, part of the south wall and above all the tower and slender 92-foot high spire. There are a few traces of an earlier Norman or Early English structure, in which Henry the priest might have officiated. During the 1830s, in an attempt to increase the seating capacity, a gallery was erected over the south aisle, but this was removed as part of a grand scheme of enlargement in 1865-66, when the nave was lengthened and a new aisle added on the north side, almost doubling the floor area. The following paragraphs trace these and later developments.

Norman Foundations

The parts of the building which are 12th-century Norman are at the base of the tower facing the nave including a half-column whose capital, carved with leaves, is Transitional. The central positioning of the tower – an unusual feature, which puts the bellringers in full view of the congregation – itself suggests the idea of a Norman foundation, as in later centuries the practice would have been to site the tower at the west end. The half-column will have formed the end of a low arcade of three arches separating the nave from the aisle to the south, perhaps more in the nature of an ambulatory. The capital seems improbably low, even allowing for the fact that the floor in that area has since been raised. A wooden cover at its foot allows one to inspect the original floor. The half-column may well have been cut down during the 19th-century alterations, either in connection with the erection of the gallery or later, to enable a new capital to be added, matching the style of the new arcade.

Capital of Norman half-column,   Norman font
carved with leaves   with cable ornamentation

The font is also Norman, with characteristic cable ornamentation at top and bottom. The base and plinth are modern, and originally it will have stood lower. In the 14th century, the current regulations required the font to be covered, but Eric Brewin observes that Cromwell's men were probably responsible for breaking the hinges and lock which secured the cover. The damage to the stone has been carefully repaired, though the marks can still be seen, and the font is generally in a good state of preservation. The lead lining has probably been renewed more than once.

14th-century Rebuilding

In the Middle Ages it was not unusual for the lord of the manor to accept responsibility for any building work on his church. Leckhampton church's enlargement in the 14th century was almost certainly undertaken by Sir John Giffard, who died in *c.*1330. The stone effigies now in the south west corner of the church are considered to be his and his wife's – see Chapter 3 for a full description.

The date of this phase of the building can be established with fair certainty from English Gothic features such as the plain vaulting of the tower and chancel and the Y-tracery of their pointed windows. 'Ballflower' moulding beneath the dripstone of a two-light window on the east wall of the chancel is also a clue. Similar work, dated precisely at 1314, is to be found at Holy Trinity, Badgeworth, and there are thousands of examples carved a decade later on Gloucester Cathedral.

Ballflower ornamentation, resembling a ball enclosed in three petals of a flower, on a dripstone high on the east wall of the chancel

The characteristic ribbed 'broach' spire also helps with the dating. This elegant method of setting an octagonal spire on to a rectangular tower is also found nearby at St Paul's, Shurdington and St Mary's, Cheltenham, also early 14th-century structures. In fact the spires of most ancient Gloucestershire churches were built before 1400 (unless they were much later additions, for example Painswick, 1632).

The ground plan of the medieval church is shown overleaf. Note the arcade of only three arches, the position of the porch, the priest's doorway to the north of the chancel and the internal entrance to the tower stairs. Both the latter openings have since been blocked up, as part of the 1865-66 alterations, and the tower is now entered from the outside. There was no vestry until the 1831-34 enlargement. The frontispiece and the illustrations on pages 20, 73 and 75 show the exterior of the church as it used to be, and parishioners will also be familiar with a water colour painting, now in the Glebe Cottages, based on a photograph taken in 1862.

The plain ribbed vaulting beneath the tower and chancel is ornamented with carved heads of angels, monks and lay men and women. Outside, two more heads of a similar style serve as stops to the hood moulding of the chancel window. These appear very life-like, and it is possible that they represent members of the 14th-century Giffard family.

23

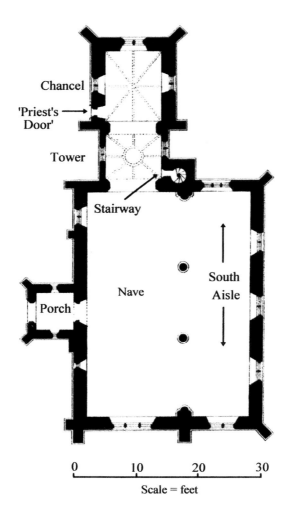

Chancel

'Priest's →
Door'

Tower

Stairway

Porch

Nave

South
Aisle

| 0 | 10 | 20 | 30 |

Scale = feet

Plan of the church as it was in the early 19th century. Only three arches separated the nave from the south aisle, and the tower steps were approached from inside. The vestry had not yet been built.

From '*Parish Churches*' by R and J A Brandon.

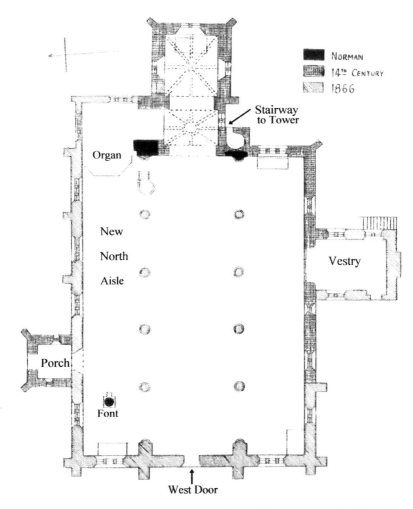

NORMAN
14TH CENTURY
1866

Stairway to Tower

Organ

New

North

Aisle

Vestry

Porch

Font

West Door

Plan after the 1866 enlargement, to approximately the same scale. New features are the lengthened nave with west door, the north aisle and the repositioned porch. The entrance to the tower steps has been altered and the 'priest's door' leading into the sanctuary blocked up. The vestry dates from 1834.

Carvings probably portraying members of the Giffard family

Christ-like carved head, formerly the central boss of the tower vault.

The sculptured Christ-like head with halo, which is now prominently placed over the chancel arch, was originally the central boss of the tower vault. It will have been taken down when a circular opening was made in the vault to enable the first set of bells to be installed in 1688. It is believed to have been rescued from obscurity and put in its present position at the time of the 1865-66 restoration. This strikingly contemporary-looking sculpture, with its elongated features, in full view of the congregation, is a unique feature of Leckhampton Church. It is matched by a similar head on the vaulting of the chancel.

What appears to be a narrow blocked-up doorway immediately to the left of the Norman half-column was probably a former entrance to the tower stairs rather than, as might be supposed, to a rood loft. There are no marks higher up the tower, or within the tower staircase itself, for an opening on to a loft, nor is there any documentary evidence that one existed.

The area of the south transept that is now known as the Lady Chapel was traditionally the reserve of the lords of the manor and their families, to whom there is an interesting and historic collection of memorial tablets. The square-headed Perpendicular east window of that chapel seems to be the model for the 19th-century copies. On either side of the window there is a stone bracket for an image. As well as an aumbry on the south wall, now fitted with a metal door, there is a recessed credence intended for the sacramental elements before consecration. Its shape is sadly marred by the memorial brass to Elizabeth Norwood; it had at one time been completely blocked up but was opened again in 1898.

The chancel, to the east of the tower, has three Decorated windows, of which the east window must later have been reconstructed and raised, as its apex is now uncomfortably close to the vaulting of the ceiling. This was probably done in the 15th century, to make room for a reredos or for an aumbry for the reserved sacrament. There is a piscina in the south wall of the chancel for use at the high altar.

The unusually lofty space above the chancel, between the groining and the roof, is lit by the windows capped with ballflower moulding, mentioned earlier. The original roof of trussed rafters with a tie-beam remains intact. In construction it resembles the upper chancel room at St John's, Elkstone, used as a pigeon loft. It is also reminiscent of the rooms over porches in the parish churches at Bishops Cleeve and Bredon, for example, which likewise date from the early 14th century. While it is possible that the space at Leckhampton was intended as accommodation for a travelling priest, there is no evidence that it has ever been used for any purpose other than as a store.

The Alterations of 1831-34

From at least the 16th century until the early 19th century the population of Leckhampton had been fairly static, with only about 100 communicants from no more than 30-40 families or households, likely to represent fewer than 200 inhabitants. The census of 1801 showed 225 adult inhabitants in the parish (the civil and ecclesiastical parishes at that time being identical). Cheltenham's growth under the Regency was parallelled in Leckhampton, where by 1831 the population had risen to 929. Moves had already been made to enlarge the church to cater for increased congregations. Tenders had been invited for alterations, and the plans came to fruition in 1834.

There had been room in the old church for only about 250 persons, including those sitting in the chancel. In 1834 the seating capacity was increased to 450 by re-pewing the whole of the body of the church and erecting a gallery on the south side. Further, to accommodate parish officials, the Rector, Canon Charles Brandon Trye, had a vestry room erected at his own expense. A new pulpit was probably also included.

According to the description in the contracts and the faculty authorising the enlargement, for which, unfortunately, no plans or drawings appear to have survived, the Norman arcade on the south side was dismantled and the stone columns replaced by three cast iron pillars supporting the gallery, which extended the full length of the south aisle. The pillars were continued upwards to join the tie-beams of the roof, while the east end rested upon the Norman half-column. A Gothic moulded cornice ornamented the lower edge of the gallery lintel. Access was by a staircase at the west end topped by an oak moulded handrail. The pews ran from east to west and were furnished with doors, each sporting a brass button. Squeezed into the low south aisle, the gallery cannot have improved the general appearance of the church and it must have been dark and cramped for those sitting in or under it. The destruction of the arcade later came to be regretted, Robert Cary Barnard describing it as 'shockingly vandalistic'.

The interior of the church had previously been simply whitewashed, but in 1831 the ceilings, walls and stone columns were puttied and plastered. It is possible to recognise the stonework remaining from that period, not only from its irregularity but also from the chiselled keying 'chips', some of which are still visible. This plastered finish remained until the time of the 1865-66 enlargement, whose specification included 'hacking off the mortar from old walls, south aisle'. Traces of whitewash remain on the vaulted ceiling of the porch, reassembled from the original stone. The later Victorian walls were built and finished in regular stone.

In 1833 an urgent repair was necessary to remedy an 'extensive and dangerous fissure in the chancel wall', and in 1838 two more buttresses were built to support the tower, as the spire was said to be considerably out of perpendicular, owing to inadequate foundations. The triangular brace at the east end of the nave, which is evident in some early photographs, probably dates from then. Moreover, the lower part of the tower walls had earlier been cut away to a bare foot in thickness in order to make more room for choir stalls, the additional weight and thickness above being supported by the corbelled arches.

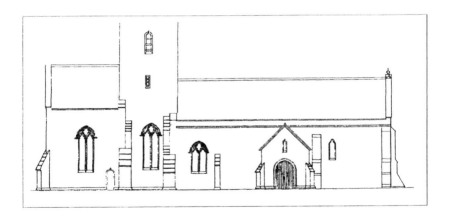

North elevation of the church before the enlargement. There was a two-light window at the foot of the tower, where the organ chamber is now.
Gloucestershire Archives

From the date of these alterations onwards, parish meetings were held regularly in the new vestry room, rather than in the church itself. The business conducted at the meetings covered both ecclesiastical and secular matters. Among the latter was the commissioning of Croome's Survey of the parish in 1835. A new parish chest was made at that time for the vestry; it is now in private possession, having been in regular use until after the Second World War.

The Enlargement of 1865-66

Cheltenham's continued expansion in the 19th century led to a further increase in Leckhampton's population. From the 929 recorded in the 1831 census it had risen to 2523 by 1861. About three-quarters of these would have lived in the area served by St Philip and St James's, where according to a religious census carried out in 1851 average attendances were five times higher than those at St Peter's. Here the figures were 100 at the morning service and 160 at evensong, plus those at Sunday School. Nevertheless, the alterations carried out in the 1830s must have been felt to be inadequate. It was therefore resolved in 1864 to remove the gallery and extend the church to the north and west.

Carved head in the porch, possibly representing the architect John Middleton

    The plans were drawn up by the noted architect John Middleton, who had already built St Mark's, Lansdown, and went on to design four more churches in Cheltenham (All Saints', Holy Apostles', St Stephen's, and St Philip and St James's), as well as making alterations to others in the county. The estimated cost of the restoration was £1575, which rose eventually to £2263 14s. 7d., to be defrayed by voluntary contributions. Among the distinguished names in the long list of those subscribing were John Middleton himself, the architect Sir Robert Smirke and Baron de Ferrieres.

Work began in 1865, and while it was in progress the schoolroom in Hall Road was licensed to be used for divine service. A visitor to the church in that year observed that 'only the chancel and the tower are now standing, the nave having been pulled down'. The work was completed in May 1866, though further additions of detail were carried out in the years immediately following, particularly in connection with the housing of the organ, described in Chapter 5.

The results of the restoration and enlargement can readily be recognised, and the plans show how much larger the church is now compared with the medieval layout. The west end was extended by some seven metres, making the whole 18 metres long, and a completely new aisle was added to the north, symmetrical with the south aisle. A doorway was included in the new west front below a high pointed window. The nave roof was raised and given a support of trussed rafters matching the new roofs of the north and south aisles; the marks of the original nave roof are still visible over the chancel arch. The old vestry was removed and a new one built in its place, combined with an organ chamber which opened directly into the south aisle. Oak wainscoting was fixed around the walls of the vestry, using wood from the gallery and also from the old pulpit. The tracery of the old windows was preserved and reproduced as far as possible. The porch was dismantled and rebuilt against the new north wall, some stones becoming inverted in the process.

Wainscoting in the vestry, taken from the old gallery

31

As part of the additional work carried out in 1871, the internal doorway leading from the ringing area to the tower steps was blocked up and a new one inserted on the outside. A small doorway in the north wall of the chancel was also blocked up.

Some decorative carving, executed by Collins and Godfrey, was added in 1907 at the expense of Baron de Ferrieres, whose other benefactions to the church are mentioned in Chapter 3. Carved heads on either side of the west door represent a mitred bishop and a crowned medieval king, and two more at the north entrance evidently portray contemporary figures, the bearded one possibly being the architect Middleton. (Similar heads are to be seen in other churches designed by Middleton, e.g. St Peter's, Clearwell.) The little statue of St Peter placed in a niche over the porch door in 1909 was donated anonymously, though it was probably also a bequest of the Baron. It was carved in Boulton and Paul's studios.

New Seating: Pew Rents

The earlier high-backed pews were replaced with what were at the time considered to be 'open and convenient seats', which offered accommodation for over 505 persons, 323 sittings being 'set apart for the use of the poorer inhabitants'.

A notice dating from 1866, and still displayed in the porch, stipulates that all sittings are free and subject to allotment by the churchwardens. Not all the seats were in fact free. According to recollections of members of the Leckhampton Women's Institute, John Ballinger, who retired in 1924 after 60 years as Sexton and Verger, had 'served at a time when pew rents were paid, and woe betide anyone who did not wait for him to conduct them to the right pew!'.

Pew rents were a guaranteed source of regular income. Indeed, when the gallery was erected, one objective had been to transfer free seats there from the body of the church, enabling some 120 additional seats to be allocated to ratepayers. At the time 42 persons were liable to have their seats allocated annually, 'except where prescriptive rights or ancient custom may make permanent allotment requisite'.

In 1896 the rents amounted to about £37. In 1907, the Leckhampton branch of the Church of England Men's Society passed a resolution that 'seats in all parish churches should be free and unappropriated'. Perhaps the debate had been prompted by a notice stating that all seats were to be free as soon as the organ voluntary began, and that visitors arriving after the start of the service could be shown to any vacant seat. Whether rented or not, the centre pews, furnished with brass name plates, were allocated to individual parishioners and their families.

Ten years later the rents were done away with and a free-will offering scheme introduced instead, which led to a doubling of income. Leckhampton was undoubtedly among the first churches locally to abolish the practice. By 1934, the Rector wrote in the parish magazine that there were no pew rents at Leckhampton, though in most if not all of the Cheltenham churches there was then such a system.

Heating

The church was heated by coal, and had been since at least the 1830s, when a new coal cupboard was made, and bills for the purchase of coal were regularly submitted. At the time of the enlargement, Messrs Haden and Son of Trowbridge supplied 'a warming apparatus and all its fittings, gratings for air openings, etc' for £53 10s. 0d. It is probably this apparatus which is evident in the corner of the Lady Chapel in the photograph on page 36. The installation of gas for lighting in 1885 would have made supplementary heating possible, but gas was not used for that purpose until 1913 when a faculty was issued for the provision of new gas radiators 'to mitigate the cold'. These proved unsatisfactory and were replaced three years later by a hot water heating apparatus and radiators.

20th-Century Improvements

The building which resulted from Middleton's extensive alterations has largely satisfied the needs of succeeding generations. Certain small alterations and improvements have been made, which reflect changing attitudes to worship, and these are described in the next chapter. Although the fabric has by no means always been in good repair or even safe, in recent years the conscientious efforts of the Churchwardens and Church Architect, reinforced by the quinquennial reviews required under the Inspection of Churches Measure, have ensured that any defects have been quickly spotted and put right.

A photograph taken in probably the 1890s shows a rather crude wooden screen filling part of the chancel arch, with a plain cross and gilded cross keys mounted on a beam above it. This structure was later removed, possibly in 1904 when two new bells were added. Marks on the inside of the arch indicate where the screen used to be.

Screen and rood beam
surmounted by a cross,
1890s

Rex Trye

In 1908-09 the spire underwent extensive renovation, including the straightening of the top ten feet, and a lightning conductor was fitted for the first time. At that time the east face of the chancel arch was reported as showing 'very ugly cracks' – possibly a reopening of the 'extensive and dangerous fissure' which had needed repair in 1833. The crack was still apparent in 1920, from the nave floor right up the face of the tower over the chancel arch, and this had increased still further when inspected in 1927.

In 1909 a pair of dormer windows was inserted near the tower. They were lengthened in 1911 and in 1964 two new pairs were fitted, in order to give better natural lighting. The Diocesan Advisor on the Care of Churches had wondered whether lime-washing might achieve the same effect, but the PCC wanted to retain the beauty of the natural Cotswold stone. All six dormer windows were double glazed in 1986 to reduce the draught which they admitted.

In other respects, the church appeared to survive the first half of the 20th century without undue deterioration. A survey in 1954 showed that the roof needed attention. In particular, the roof timbers of the chancel and the porch needed treatment against death watch beetle; the north-facing roofs were re-tiled some years later. Minor internal alterations included the removal of the front pews, making an easier entrance from the vestry. The area of the baptistry was paved with new stone and the font moved a little further away from the north wall.

In 1967 the medieval aumbry behind the high altar was revived and, in keeping with modern liturgical trends, a nave altar designed by Robert Paterson was introduced, faced with Westmorland stone slabs, with a 4-inch thick Portland stone top. The earlier choir stalls (once described in a parish magazine as 'ugly and inadequate') were replaced by others in light oak, standing at first near the organ in the north aisle but later moved to the back of the church. To accommodate a new long altar rail, the pew frontals were taken away and the pulpit moved. Draft-excluding wooden screens which had formed a lobby inside the north doorway were also removed at this time.

The last series of major repairs was carried out in 1971-72. It was reported that 'only a line of pews prevents the floor of the north aisle ... from total collapse', and cracks were found once again in the fabric of the tower and spire, needing urgent repair. The spire was completely overhauled and reinforced with concrete ring-beams. The bells were also in a parlous state; their recasting and rehanging are described in Chapter 4.

The Future

Over the centuries the building and its furnishings have undergone many changes. Not only the structure itself but seating, choir stalls, altars, the organ, bells, windows, lighting and heating, monuments and memorials – all have been affected by shifting trends in worship and the needs and expectations of the congregation. Some innovations have been controversial and a few may have been regretted afterwards, but in general they have soon come to be accepted.

Further changes are inevitable in the 21st century, but they should be seen against that background. Future historians will no doubt be able to put them into perspective.

The interior in about 1900. Note the reredos at the high altar, the monuments since repositioned, the triangular wall-brace, gas lighting, heating stove and name plates on the pews.

The interior of the church today, from the same viewpoint. Clerestory windows provide extra light, and an altar has been introduced into the nave. Victorian 'clutter' has been removed.

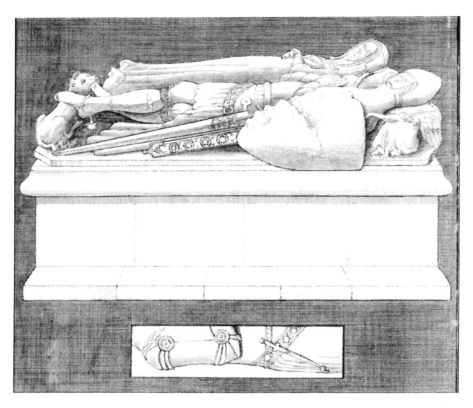

Effigies of Sir John Giffard, who built the church in the early 14th century, and his wife. When moved to the south-west corner of the building they were transposed, and Sir John is now on his wife's right. The engraving, from Lysons's *Collection of Gloucestershire Antiquities*, shows the knight's intricately carved armour.

3
MONUMENTS, MEMORIALS AND FURNISHINGS

The Monuments

Some fifty memorial plaques and tablets are displayed on the interior walls of the church, and other names are inscribed on stone slabs on the floor. Among the earliest are those commemorating members of the families of the lords of the manor, but there is also an interesting selection of Victorian memorials to people with Indian Empire connections, who led adventurous and sometimes tragic lives.

By far the oldest monument is the pair of carved stone effigies which are generally believed to represent Sir John Giffard, who died in about 1330, and his lady (see opposite). It is now tucked away in the south west corner of the church but has been moved at least twice before. Plans drawn by John Middleton in 1865 suggest that it was next to the north wall of the tower, but he had it moved to join the memorials to the Norwoods and the Tryes, lying east-west at the foot of the Norman half-column. A photograph taken during the First World War shows it placed against the south wall of the chapel, and when this was rearranged in 1920 the monument was moved to its present position.

The pillows supporting their heads are held up by angels; the knight's feet are supported by lions and his lady's by dogs. The knight's right leg is crossed over his left. It is sometimes suggested that this means that he was a Crusader. Whether or not that is so, in this case it is probably just a flattering compliment, as Sir John Giffard lived after the last of the Crusades had been waged. Though no coat of arms is carved on his shield, his effigy is in other respects considered one of the best of that period in the county and the details of the armour, sword and scabbard are of particular interest. Sir John was originally to his lady's left. For some reason, when the effigies were last moved they were transposed. Middleton states that both figures had originally been decorated with painting, but no traces of colour remain.

There is one outstanding example of a memorial brass. It shows Elizabeth Norwood, of the Lygon family of Madresfield Court in Worcestershire, who died in 1598 aged 50, with her husband William and their nine sons and two daughters. Their costumes offer a good illustration of what was worn by the gentry towards the end of the reign of Queen Elizabeth I.

Rubbing of the brass memorial to William Norwood's wife Elizabeth Lygon
Amy Woolacott

Near the font is another effigy, which was moved indoors from the churchyard at the end of the 19th century to save it from further weathering. It represents a priest, in mass vestments characteristic of the late 15th or early 16th centuries, holding a chalice in folded hands.

A number of worn flagstones near the vestry are engraved with memorials to early members of the Norwood family. Of particular note is that to the above-mentioned William Norwood, *d.* 1632, and his grandson Colonel Henry Norwood, *d.* 1689. On the wall of the Lady

Chapel is a memorial to William's eldest son Richard, who predeceased him in 1630.

Other inscriptions recorded by 18th-century antiquaries now seem to have been removed or perhaps in some cases were covered over when the war memorial chapel was fashioned in 1921. These included memorials to Francis Norwood, *d.* 1682, and his wife Judith, who produced nine sons and nine daughters, all but two reaching adulthood.

Other names worthy of recording include:

- The Reverend Robert Jones, Rector from 1654 to 1707, who died aged 84 (see also page 13).

- Charles Brandon Trye, FRS, *d.* 1811. He was Senior Surgeon to the Gloucester Infirmary and is also commemorated by an imposing monument in Gloucester Cathedral.

- Sir Francis Henry Drake, Bart, *d.* 1839 aged 83. He is stated to have been the last surviving male descendant of 'the great circumnavigator'. *Burke's Peerage,* however, lists his uncle of the same name, who died in 1794, as the last baronet (and even he was not a direct but a collateral descendant, the great Sir Francis having died childless). Leckhampton's Sir Francis assumed the title on his uncle's death, but the legitimacy of his claim is considered doubtful, the marriage of his father (later Vice-Admiral) Francis William Drake to Grace America Gredhill, of Newfoundland, being of questionable validity. He evidently felt himself morally entitled to the baronetcy, however, and perpetuated his claim in his memorial, which is surmounted by the Drake family crest.

- Charles Whitmore of the Bengal Civil Service, *d.* 1844 in the East Indies, aged 36. The deaths are also recorded of his three infant children in India and in Egypt.

- Lieutenant Franklin Knight Kirby, died of typhus in the Crimea in 1855, aged 19.

- The wife and children of Henry Lloyd Evans of the Bombay Infantry, who died in 1857 during the Indian Mutiny, crushed by the fall of the roof of the barracks at Cawnpore. Mrs Evans's brother Charles Henry Fitzroy Gambier was mortally wounded during the assault on Delhi later that year, aged 23.

- Sir Edward Smirke, *d.* 1875, buried at Kensal Green. Sir Edward was a barrister with an interest in mining in the Duchy of Cornwall. His architect brother, Sir Robert, is buried in the churchyard.
- William Joseph Gale, *d.* 1877 aged 19. Perhaps the most poignant inscription of all: 'near Nazareth ... he fell among robbers'.
- George Backhouse Witts, *d.* 1912. He was a notable local dignitary and an antiquarian with an interest in the history of Leckhampton.
- Elsie Holt, *d.* 1913 aged 24, buried at sea west of Morocco.

The Ten Commandments

There are two matching stone tablets, high up on the west wall, one listing the Ten Commandments, the other the Apostles' Creed and the Lord's Prayer. These were paid for by subscription in 1849-50 and were then placed on the east wall of the chancel, where traces of their outline can still be made out. They were moved during the 1865-66 enlargement. Earlier, the Ten Commandments and Lord's Prayer had been painted on wooden boards which, together with a coat of arms, were 'cleaned, varnished and touched up' in 1833. It is not clear whether the latter was the royal one (as at St Mary's, Charlton Kings) or that of the Norwoods or Tryes, as it has not survived. However, it was evidently still there in 1848, when one shilling was charged for putting it up.

War Memorials

The First World War

As a memorial to those who gave their lives in the First World War an altar was added and a new floor laid in what is now the Lady Chapel. The locker placed in the aumbry was included in the work, which was dedicated on 4 April 1921. As late as 1928 there were still plans to have the names of the fallen engraved near the altar, but in the following year they were inscribed in a book of remembrance. With a few discrepancies, the names also appear on the Parish War Memorial in Church Road and have been painted on a board that hangs near the font.

The triptych that now stands behind the altar is a reproduction of the *Adoration of the Mystic Lamb* by Jan and Hubert Van Eyck, of which the original is in Ghent Cathedral in Belgium. It was given in 1932 and had formerly been the property of the clergyman cousin of the then Rector, Archdeacon Sears. It was removed after the Second World War and was for some time stored in the vestry, but has recently been returned to its previous position. To preserve their modesty, someone has crudely painted animal skins on the figures of Adam and Eve.

The Second World War

The wish to create a lasting memorial to those who fell in the Second World War served as an incentive to make improvements to the chancel, whose Victorian appearance will have been out of keeping with the spirit of the times. This involved the removal of the reredos evident in the photograph on page 36, given in 1890 by members of the Julian family, of Gwynfa, Moorend Park Road, and the replacement of a marble-topped altar, a legacy of an alteration carried out in 1899. A new high altar was made corresponding in width with the east window. The tiled floor was repaved in Northleach stone, Leckhampton's quarries having ceased production in 1926.

The new War Memorial Chapel, complete with a silver cross and candlesticks, was dedicated on St George's Day 1950. Appropriate words are inscribed in one of the flagstones by the altar rail. (Latterly, the chancel and tower area have come to be called instead the Corpus Christi Chapel.)

The Stained Glass Windows

All the windows have stained glass, dating from about 1858 to 1908. Because they were mostly separate gifts and bequests, they do not illustrate any consistent theme, unlike the glass in some medieval churches, and some even duplicate each other. Nevertheless, all repay closer examination. Their subjects as listed below are based in part on a catalogue prepared by the late Robert Paterson. The numbers relate to the those on the plan overleaf.

1. Porch West   (Jacob) 'This is none other than the house of God'
2. Porch East   St Peter

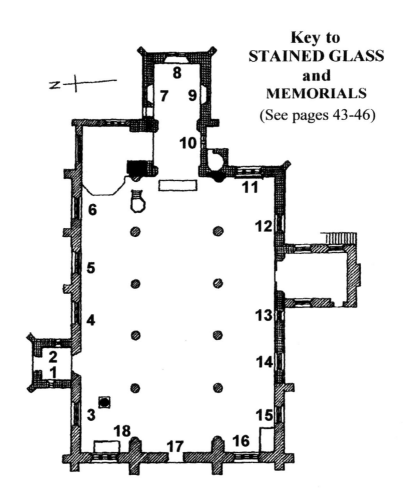

N

8

7　9

10

11

6

12

5

4

13

2
1

14

3

15

18

17　16

3. North Aisle	The presentation in the Temple
4.	Christ the preacher
5.	The Good Samaritan
6.	Christ at Bethany with Mary and Martha
7. Chancel North	Visitation of the shepherds
8. Chancel East	St Peter and St John
9. Chancel South	Three miracles • Suffer the little children
10. Tower South	Pax vobiscum • the Ascension
11. South Aisle East	*Above* St Elizabeth • St Margaret
	Main The Good Shepherd • Jairus's daughter •
	Of such is the Kingdom of God
12. South Aisle South	Faith • Hope • Charity
13. South Aisle	The Good Shepherd
14.	Suffer the little children
15.	St Michael • a warrior(?) • David and Goliath
16. South Aisle West	St Matthew • the Transfiguration • St Mark
17. Nave West	The Nativity • Christ in Majesty(?) • the Baptism
18. North Aisle West	St Luke (bull) • St John (eagle) • St Luke •
	the raising of Lazarus • St John

The dedications of most of the windows are indicated either on the glass itself or on a plaque nearby. The two windows in the porch, Nos 1 & 2, and also Nos 13 and 14 in the south aisle, were given by Baron de Ferrieres, a former Mayor and MP for Cheltenham and a great benefactor to the town and Leckhampton church. He and his father are buried in the churchyard. No 3 is in memory of members of the Fenwick family, of Thirlestaine House. Nos 4 and 5 in the north aisle were given in memory of Dr Disney Launder Thorp by his widow, Mrs Eleanor Thorp of Lypiatt Lodge. She was a local benefactress, among other things leaving money to provide 'coals and warm clothing for poor people in the parish of Leckhampton'. She also paid for the conversion of the Gordon Lamp from gas to electricity in 1899.

The conspicuous east window of the chancel, No 8, is a memorial to the Reverend Lawrence Harrison, curate at St Peter's 1856 - 1859 before becoming priest-in-charge of St Philip and St James's. The glass in No 9 is the oldest, dedicated to Joseph Stanton who died in 1858, and may therefore have been installed before the 1866 enlargement. No 10 commemorates Alexander Shirer of South Court, for many years a churchwarden, and No 11 is in memory of his two daughters, Elizabeth and Margaret. No 12 commemorates the aforementioned Reverend Charles Brandon Trye. All three windows on the west wall, Nos 16-18, are memorials to members of the family of the Reverend Thomas Longworth, related to the Tryes by marriage.

In 1928 a bequest of £200 was intended to provide a stained glass window in memory of General Augustus Halifax Ferryman and his wife. However, as by then all the windows had been replaced with stained glass, the money was diverted to provide electric lighting for the first time. Until then, the lighting had been by gas, installed in 1885 and improved in 1907 by the provision of 'incandescent burners'. The installation of electricity was completed in 1930.

The Pulpit

Panels from an earlier pulpit, presumably the one which was made at the time of the 1831-34 alterations, were in 1871 added to the wainscoting in the vestry. The photograph on page 36 shows that its place was taken by what amounts to a large lectern.

The present pulpit dates from 1913 and is a memorial to Mary Trye and Eleanor Meredith, daughters of Canon Charles Brandon Trye. It was designed along traditional Gothic lines by Leonard Barnard and made from oak grown in the grounds of Leckhampton Court. It has six panels decorated with linenfold carving and surmounted by intertwined vine leaves and fruit. At the corners are exquisitely carved figures of angels playing ancient musical instruments – cymbals, lute, lyre, shawm and psaltery.

At the same time, Leonard Barnard had designed a reredos for the high altar and wrought iron gates for the lych gate, but these plans were not taken further.

Details of three of the carved angels on the pulpit, playing cymbals, psaltery and shawm

The Liturgical Plate

The church is endowed with a variety of plate for liturgical use – chalices, patens, flagons and salvers – most of it elegant but functional and of no special interest. The more historic items have been passed to Gloucester Cathedral Treasury for safe keeping. The oldest are a chalice and matching paten, probably both dating from 1574 according to expert opinion, the latter bearing the inscription '1634, Lackhampton' (*sic*). A flagon, dating from 1619 and inscribed for the use of Leckhampton Parish Church, was presented by Sir Richard Norwood in 1688 (the same year that his uncle gave the bells). A small silver salver on four feet, dating from 1757, was a gift of the Reverend John Trye in 1765, and an octagonal salver for altar bread, probably made in Edinburgh in 1759, is inscribed as a gift of one George Caldwell in 1830. Richard Norwood's flagon and John Trye's salver were stolen from the vestry in 1976. After being given up for lost, they were found in the Hatherley Brook some three years later.

The lectern

The Lectern

The brass eagle lectern was given in memory of G B Witts's step-daughter Caroline Vavasour, who died in 1906.

The Clock

The clock was installed in 1948 in memory of William Alfred Salsbury and his daughter, Dr Janet Mary Salsbury. It has no exterior dial, as it was felt at the time that this would be inappropriate on the ancient tower. The mechanism strikes on the church bells, using a version of the Westminster chimes. The family had earlier presented the organ to the church.

4

THE BELLS

The bells of Leckhampton church are well known throughout the ringing world, thanks largely to the enthusiasm of its team of ringers. A number of ringing methods are named after it, such as Leckhampton Delight, Leckhampton Place Minor and Leckhampton Surprise Major.

The earliest bells date from 1688, when Abraham Rudhall of Gloucester cast a ring of five which he installed as a gift of Colonel Henry Norwood. Abel Rudhall added a treble in 1746. By 1833 the old fifth was cracked and the fittings were barely usable. It was recast by John Rudhall, who described it as a 'clean cast good sounding one', and all six bells were rehung in that year. The frame was in a very bad state, however, and later there was concern over the bells' safety. By 1857 the tenor appears to have cracked, and in the following year C and G Mears recast it, Rudhalls having gone out of business.

By the end of the 19th century the bells were again in a poor state and could not be rung for Queen Victoria's 80th birthday in May 1899. Major restoration was carried out in 1904. The old second, which had become cracked, was recast by Taylors of Loughborough. Two new trebles were added, in memory of Isabel Richardson, the widow of the Reverend George Richardson, former Vicar of Kilburn, Yorkshire; she is buried at Leckhampton. For many years afterwards it was the custom to ring a commemorative peal on the date of their dedication, 4 April. The family made similar gifts elsewhere, including seven bells at St Matthias's at Malvern Link, where Mrs Richardson lived for a time.

In 1935 the whole octave was rehung on ball bearings by Mears and Stainbank, after 'vital parts of the mechanism had very nearly worn through and might have given way at any moment'. Unfortunately the old frame was retained, and during the 1960s it too became dangerous. The action of the bells deteriorated and they were rehung in 1972, at a cost of £3,300. The third, seventh and tenor were recast by Taylors and the whole ring was retuned and hung in a new frame. Defects were revealed in the tower and two reinforced concrete beams were inserted, while the whole tower and spire were repointed and strengthened.

The two bells remaining from 1688 (the fifth and sixth) turned out to be cracked in the crown. Since they were the oldest bells but one in the diocese, with the coat of arms of James II on the side – a very rare feature on Rudhall's work – it was decided that one of them should be preserved. The old sixth was placed in the care of Cheltenham Museum and a new bell cast in its place, while the old fifth was recast.

The coat of arms of King James II on the old sixth bell
Courtesy of Cheltenham Art Gallery and Museums

Leckhampton now possesses a well-tuned light ring of eight 20th-century bells, the tenor weighing 9 cwt (476 kilogrammes). Their specification is given at Appendix C on page 68. Some 350 peals have been rung on them as well as many more quarter peals as a prelude to services. According to Bob Harley, who was born in No 1 Church Cottages when his father was the sexton, for evening services in the 1920s and 1930s the bells were chimed from the chamber above (now the clock room).

Much of the credit for the status of ringing at Leckhampton is due to the late Eric Taylor, who became captain in 1969, and his family, five of whom took part in a peal rung in 2006 to celebrate the 80th birthday of his widow, Helen. Earlier teams had displayed similar longevity and dedication. According to the parish magazine of May 1930, the band of ringers which performed that year's commemorative peal for Isabel Richardson was, with two exceptions, the same as it had been in 1904. They may of course have been fortified by a 10-gallon barrel of cider kept at that time in the boiler room, which, as Bob Harley recalls, was frequented by members of the choir as well as ringers.

5

THE ORGAN

There is a strong oral tradition that singing at St Peter's used to be accompanied in the gallery by a barrel organ which played a limited number of tunes, and that this was later replaced by harp and violins. Certainly a barrel organ existed as early as 1832, when the gallery was being erected, and accounts were rendered for 'putting up the organ' and 'altering seats at the organ', while in 1841 a bill showed that the barrel had been repaired. The fate of this instrument is not known.

By the second half of the 19th century pipe organs were becoming more fashionable, and the enlargement of 1865-66 included provision for such an instrument, sited at the front of the vestry. This arrangement proved unsatisfactory and in 1871 the present organ chamber was built at the east end of the north aisle. As a consequence, the area devoted to the vestry could be enlarged, and it is now entered directly from the south aisle through a door in a glazed wooden partition.

The instrument which Leckhampton acquired in 1866 had previously been in the 'temporary church' (a corrugated iron building erected in Clarence Street in 1859 for use while Cheltenham Parish Church was being renovated). It was built by the Cheltenham firm of Henry Williams and had two manuals, pedals and at least 15 stops. This organ was remodelled in preparation for its repositioning in 1871, in the process obscuring a memorial. For a time, until the new organ chamber was completed, it stood in the north aisle, where the choir now sits.

As a second-hand instrument, the organ must have left something to be desired. A repair fund was already in being in 1873-75, and in 1888 a more extensive restoration was undertaken and the pipes were painted. We get an idea how it looked from the photograph overleaf.

Further work became necessary some twenty years later, and in 1909 tenders were obtained for the organ's restoration or replacement. One possibility considered was the offer of the organ then in use at St Paul's Training College in part exchange. An appeal fund was opened in 1911, but Mr R T Morgan, the organist of St Mary Redcliffe, having examined the existing organ, recommended a scheme of reconstruction.

The original organ, with painted pipes

In 1913 a faculty was issued for the organ to be restored and enlarged and for the construction of a Quebec oak case. This work was carried out by Messrs Liddiatt and Sons, to whom the parish authorities complained that the bellows were noisy. These were worked by hand, and the organ-blower was paid 2 guineas a quarter (as against the organist's £21 and the verger's 4 guineas).

Today's 3-manual organ, an entirely new instrument built by Hill, Norman and Beard, was presented in 1936 in memory of Mrs Mary Elizabeth Salsbury and her daughter Ethel Maria, members of a family that had played a prominent part in Cheltenham's musical life. The action is electro-pneumatic. There were originally 1700 pipes and 36 speaking stops, and its specification (since altered slightly – see

Appendix D on page 69) had received the approval of the organist at the Chapels Royal, Sir Stanley Roper, who was the performer at the opening concert.

In 1974 the organ was renovated, the action renewed and minor changes made. There had been a plan instead to build a new organ sited on a raised platform over the west door. Although this would have been acoustically more satisfactory, it was ruled out in view of the cost and other more pressing work, described earlier. Some documents have recently come to light which include an illustration of how the arrangement might have looked.

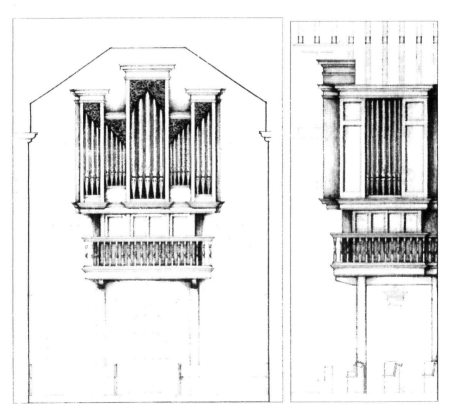

Artist's impression of the organ, to be re-erected in a gallery above the west door, c.1974. The project was never realised.

It is easy to see why this move was wanted. The chancel had been rearranged in 1967, when the free-standing altar was installed. The choirstalls were eventually moved to the back of the church (which explains why the four light oak pews at the west end are raised higher than those in front). Needless to say, this arrangement did not make for easy communication between organist and singers, and in 1980 the choir was moved yet again to its present position next to the organ. In the circumstances this probably remains the best compromise.

In 2000 Nicholsons of Malvern carried out a complete restoration of the instrument, replacing perished and cracked leatherwork and cleaning the pipes. The cost was a little over £25,000, most of which was raised in the course of one day by a special fundraising appeal.

The pipework of the swell and great organs in today's instrument

From St Peter's organ appeal, 2000

6
THE CHURCHYARD

God's Acre

The earliest burials were in the area immediately surrounding the church, but the churchyard has been enlarged several times and now occupies over three acres. Its capacity was first increased in 1856, and it was most recently extended on the south side in 1948, with the incorporation of a small part of Church Meadow.

There are examples of rustic headstones as well as some more elaborate chest tombs. For a country churchyard there is also an unusually rich collection of graves of 19th-century Cheltonians, some of them renowned nationally. Like the memorials inside the church, they are a reflection of the wider social history of Cheltenham.

Eleven tombstones from the 17th and 18th centuries are listed by English Heritage as Grade II structures. Also listed are some extremely unusual carved stones, on either side of the porch, probably dating from the 14th century. Now in a very dilapidated condition, some were found when the foundations of the new nave and north aisle were being dug and others were moved from elsewhere in the churchyard. The nine to the west of the porch are coffin lids, on five of which can be seen traces of embossed crosses. On the east side is an effigy with short robes and no headdress, evidently of a man, while the others, in longer robes, represent women. One appears to be holding a heart and all four rest their feet on dogs. Given their likely date, it is possible that the effigies represent members of the family of Sir John Giffard.

The Cotswold stone of most of the early graves is badly eroded and the inscriptions are difficult to read. However, plans of the churchyard drawn up in 1914 by Leonard Barnard show that the earliest belongs to Ralph Crump, at that time a common local surname, who died in 1670. Among well-established local names are Ballinger, Barrett, Caudle, Cherrington, Fletcher, Hall, Hicks, Joyner, Pearman and Townsend.

14th-century effigies and coffin lids on either side of the porch

Frcm Leckhampton Court there are the Tryes, both lords of the manor and clergy, and John Hargreaves and his wife, née Edith Platt.

Many of the 19th-century and early 20th-century graves are of people who had lived outside Leckhampton. (Special arrangements also allowed residents of St Philip and St James's parish to be buried at St Peter's.) Some had come to Cheltenham on retirement, perhaps having served in the Indian Army or East India Company. It is likely that they were buried at Leckhampton because there was no space left in the graveyards of the churches they had attended in the town. In 1918, for example, burials of non-parishioners at Leckhampton outnumbered those of parishioners by four to one.

Among the many military graves, those of at least 30 generals and seven admirals have been counted. Three holders of the Victoria Cross have memorials: Commander Cecil William Buckley RN, from the Crimean War, the holder of the first VC to be gazetted; William Fraser McDonnell from the Indian Mutiny, a member of the Bengal Civil Service, who came to live in Cheltenham and died in 1894, one of the few civilians to hold the award; and Major Douglas Reynolds from the First World War.

On a granite cross is recorded the death of Dr Edward Wilson, formerly of the Crippetts, who died in 1912 as Chief Scientist on Scott's South Polar Expedition.

Other notables are:

- the above-mentioned Baron de Ferrieres
- Sir Robert Smirke, architect of the British Museum, Eastnor Castle and Shire Hall, Gloucester
- Evangeline Butler, the 5-year-old daughter of the social reformer Josephine Butler
- Fanny Duberly, the officers' darling from the Crimean War, who witnessed the Charge of the Light Brigade and who also wrote about her experiences during the Indian Mutiny
- the musician John Barnett, once described as the 'father of English opera', though his work goes unperformed today, and his son Domenico, who taught music at The Ladies' College

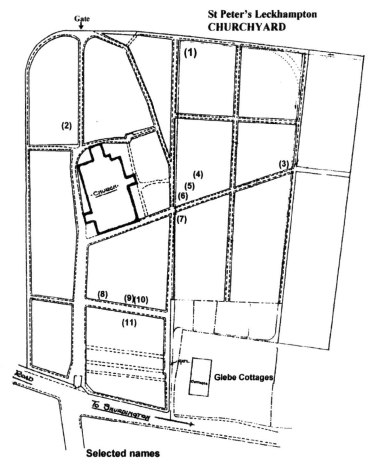

St Peter's Leckhampton
CHURCHYARD

Gate

CHURCH

Glebe Cottages

To Shurdington

Selected names

1. Barnett   2. Purser   3. Wilson   4. McDonnell VC   5. Wyatt   6. Duberly

7. Reynolds VC   8. Smirke   9. De Ferrières   10. Butler   11. Buckley VC

Note. Many of the names and inscriptions on the tombstones have been recorded by Julian Rawes and can be found on the Leckhampton Local History Society's website <www.llhs.org.uk>. Click on 'Family History Research' and 'Tombstone inscriptions at St Peter's Church'.

- the Reverend Joseph Fenn, sometime Vicar of Christ Church
- Thomas Billings, the developer of the Park Estate
- John Fletcher, a former Parish Clerk, and his successor for 45 years Neighbour Pearman, who was also manager of Leckhampton Quarries.
- Nathaniel Smith, who built the house named Wychbury (now demolished) in Moorend Road
- Barnard George Thompson, Headmaster of Leckhampton School (and after whom Thompson Drive is named)
- Frank Webley, a photographer who had a shop at the end of Church Road and produced postcards of the area, and whose wife later ran the post office

In the chapter on Leckhampton in Arthur Mee's *Gloucestershire* he refers to 'three pathetic wooden crosses from the Great War'. They commemorate local men who had died in action or in one case (as the Parish War Memorial shows) as a prisoner of war: Alfred Enoch MM, and Harold Summers, both of the Glosters, and Victor Hunt, of the Inniskilling Fusiliers. The original crosses, sent over from Flanders, had rotted away and have been replaced by new ones.

What must surely be Leckhampton's longest-living inhabitant ever, Richard Purser, who is buried near the north-east corner of the church, was allegedly 111 when he died in 1868. He was described in a letter to *The Times* as 'the oldest man in England'.

The Glebe Cottages

According to a document of 1683, a labourer's cottage, commonly known as Church House, at that time stood between the church and the road. This will have been the 'new church house' towards which Roger Norwood had left timber in 1512. It is also shown on the Enclosure Award Map of 1778 and on Croome's map of 1835.

The building was pulled down presumably in 1856 when the piece of ground that surrounded it was added to the churchyard. Some of the stone will have been utilised in building the 'Church Cottages', intended as two separate dwellings for the verger and the sexton. Although these are separate functions, the one concerned with duties during services, the other with the care of the church and churchyard, they were later combined. The last holder of these offices was Bert Newman, who was 'churchyard attendant', also serving as parish clerk. Since his retirement in 1981 no one has been appointed to carry out any of these duties full time.

The Glebe Cottages

By the 1970s the cottages had fallen into disrepair and had become uninhabitable. However, they were renovated and are now used by the Sunday School and as a meeting place for a variety of church activities, some of which had previously been held in a room in the rectory. The transformation of what are today known as the 'Glebe Cottages' was carried out almost entirely by voluntary labour and was completed in 1978.

The Avenue of Lime Trees

The lofty avenue of lime trees leading from the lych gate to the church dominates the approach to the church. They must be almost 180 years old, as the accounts for 1827 show a bill of 6 shillings for the purchase of lime trees, and there is every likelihood that those are the ones standing today. The lych gate was built in 1893.

The trees in the avenue to the east of the church, linking it with Leckhampton Court, may be even older. An illustration in Atkyns's *Ancient and Present State of Gloucestershire* published in 1712 showed such an avenue. In 1969 four trees at either end of the church, some of them elms, had to be felled, as the roots of some were affecting the foundations, and others were virtually hollow and threatened to collapse on to the building.

The 1894 catalogue for the sale of Leckhampton Court referred to a 'fine avenue of limes diverging from the Northern Drive to a gateway entrance leading to Leckhampton church'. This gate still exists, though it is no longer in use. Its closure prevents the risk of cattle getting into the churchyard, as they did in 1910, trampling over a newly levelled area.

It used to be the custom at Rogationtide, at least until the 1950s, for the clergy and congregation to go in procession from the church along the avenue of lime trees to the terrace of Leckhampton Court, where a service of Blessing of the Crops was held. This practice reflected the close links which had existed between church and Court over the centuries, and that avenue will have been used by the family of the lords of the manor to pass to and from the church.

7

MISCELLANY

Under the Pews

Beneath each end of the pew seats are screwed pairs of L-shaped wooden runners, about 11½ inches (30cm) apart. The inquisitive visitor may find similar runners under the pews of a few other churches. Locally there are isolated examples at Painswick and Charlton Kings, and Cirencester parish church also has some under virtually every pew. Ingenious explanations have been put forward, such as that they were designed to accommodate a top hat. However, the brim of a top hat would have been of the wrong shape and dimensions to fit the narrow groove in the runners. A visit to Tetbury parish church offers an explanation of their true purpose. Under several of its box pews are runners into which a lockable wooden drawer has been slid, suitable for holding prayer and hymn books belonging to the regular occupants. Another example, from Somerset, is illustrated below. There can therefore be no doubt that when the new pews were installed in 1866 provision was made for drawers of this kind, though there is no evidence that they were ever fitted.

Runners under pew at St Peter's and drawer at Martock parish church, Somerset

Painting of the Holy Family

Above the north entrance is a painting of the Madonna and Child, with St Anne or Elizabeth and the infant John the Baptist, to whom Jesus gives a sign of blessing. In a doorway on the left stands an older male figure, presumably Joseph. The painting, in the manner of the early Ita'ian masters, is by one Luigi Barone, who executed it in Naples in 1843. It was given to the church in 1945 by the Reverend Dr Edmund Godfrey Burr, formerly Vicar of Bude, who came to live in Cheltenham on retirement and is buried at Leckhampton. It was originally hung over the chancel arch, facing the congregation, but soon afterwards was removed to a position high on the wall at the west end of the south aisle. It was rehung in its present position in 1986.

The Mass Dial

On a buttress supporting the south side of the chancel is a dial scratched into the stone. It has 24 radial lines, of which those pointing to the top and bottom are crossed by a number of horizontal marks. This is a mass dial, once used to indicate the times of services. The hole in the centre will have served as a pivot for a cursor, pointing to the appropriate hour. It is not to be confused with a sundial, whose geometrical layout would be quite different. (Quite separately, there is a sundial gnomon on the same side of the tower, surprisingly high up and impossible to read.) Such mass dials are generally found on churches of the 13th-15th centuries and may take a variety of forms. At St Mary's, Charlton Kings, a roughly semi-circular dial, now built into the south wall near the westernmost buttress, may date back to c.1190.

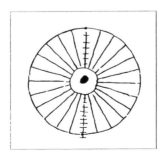

Mass dial on a buttress to the south of the chancel

Dedication Cross

Outside the chancel, by the south window, a dedication cross, 8½ inches (21.5 cm) across, is incised into the stone. By contrast, the large cross on the inside of the east wall of the south aisle is probably no more than a cross from a tombstone which was incorporated when making good the wall during renovation.

The Weathercock

The gilded weathercock, which crowns the church spire and attracts the eye as it catches the sunlight, dates from 1828 when it replaced an earlier one. The cost of removing the old one and putting on the new came to 2s 6d (12½ pence). A weathercock is shown in the 1712 print of Leckhampton Court.

Lighting the Way to the Church

In the buttress on the north west angle of the porch there is a little notch cut into the stone. According to Leonard Barnard, it was originally meant to hold a torch to light the way from the road. Much more recently, a lamp bracket was fitted over the porch doorway, incorporating the crossed keys of St Peter, and reminiscent of the ironwork on the Parish Hall. It was probably designed to hold a gas mantle but now supports an electric lamp.

Lighting the way to the church has always presented a problem. In 1907 Captain Elwes of Leckhampton Court and Canon Proctor had lamps erected between Leckhampton Court Lodge and the entrance to the church, in an attempt to improve the situation. Nevertheless, attendances at evensong were poor, as the church still stood some distance from the tram-road and its electric lights. The rector remarked in the parish magazine that more than one lady 'would not allow her servant to attend church on account of that dark lane'.

For a more conveniently located place of worship, a large piece of ground opposite the Malvern Inn was said to have been secured. The ill-defined plans came to nothing, however, and the site is now occupied by shops. Instead, in 1910, a plot was identified on the corner of Pilley Lane, but the owner of the land was unwilling to sell.

APPENDIX A

LIST OF INCUMBENTS AND PATRONS

Date	Incumbent's Name	Patron
- 1162 - 1199 -	Henry	
- 1270 -	Fulk of Penebrig	
1286 - 1287	Walter Burdon	Sir Adam Despenser,
1287 - ?	Adam of York	Sir Adam Despenser,
1297 - 1303	John Gamage	Lady Joan Despenser
c.1347 - d. 1349	William of Eyleworth	
1349 - 1354	William of Blechesdon	Johanna Giffard
1354 - ?	William of Farendon	Johanna Giffard
	Master Edmond Frowceter, DD (Curate)	John Norwood
1546	Sir[1] Richard Banystur (?)	
d. 1549 -	Sir Robert Fynche	
1549 - d. 1570	Sir Rhys Jones	Ralph Norwood
1570 - d. 1612	Ralph Gynes (but absent in at least 1572)	William Badger and John Slaughter, granted by William Norwood
1571/2	Anthony Higgins, clerk	William Rogers
1620	Humphrey Stodard	
1620 - 1637	Henry Williams	
1647[2]	Rowland Crosby	
1650	Humphrey Randell, MA	
1654 - d. 1707	Robert Jones, MA, clerk	Francis Norwood
1707 - d. 1734	Thomas Norwood, MA.	Arthur Charlett STP[3]
1735 - d. 1738	John Brown, MA, clerk	William Norwood
1738	Richard Arthur, BA, clerk	William Norwood
1738 - 1744	Clement Headington, BA	William Norwood
1744 - d. 1766	John Trye, BA	William Norwood
1767 - d. 1825	Edward Draper, clerk	Charles Norwood
1825 - 1830	Thomas Commeline, MA	Henry Norwood Trye I
1830 -1884	Charles Brandon Trye, MA	Henry Norwood Trye I
1884 - d. 1928	Reginald Edward Trye, MA[4]	Henry Norwood Trye II

Date	Incumbent's Name	Patron
1895 - 1904	William Clifford Aston, MA[5]	Henry Norwood Trye II
1904 - 1912	Henry Proctor, MA[5]	Mrs Nevile Wyatt
1912 - 1915	Frederick William Bidwell, MA[5]	Bishop of Gloucester
1915 - 1921	Augustine John Hodson, MA[5 6]	"
1921 - 1928	Francis Reginald Standfast, MA[5]	"
1928 - 1938	Frederick William Sears, MA[7]	"
1938 - 1940	Henry James Hensman, AKC[8]	"
1941 - 1954	Eric William Bradley Cordingly, AKC[9]	"
1955 - d. 1966	Edgar John White, BA	"
1966 - d. 1970	Geoffrey Coleridge Ford	"
1970 - 1981	Eric Walter Brewin, MA	"
1982 - 1994	George Robert Henry Smith	"
1995 - 2002	Adrian Berry, MA	"
2003 -	Paul Wilkinson[10]	"

Footnotes

1. A form of address for the clergy
2. The living was sequestered in that year
3. Professor of Sacred Theology; he was Master of University College, Oxford
4. His living was sequestered in 1885, after which he lived away from the parish
5. During the sequestration, 1886 - 1929, these were curates-in-charge
6. The first Bishop of Tewkesbury, 1938 - 1955
7. Archdeacon of Cheltenham from 1932
8. Associate of King's College, London
9. Bishop of Thetford, 1964 -1976
10. Priest-in-charge

The names of the earlier incumbents are mostly taken from the 'Hockaday Abstracts' held in the Gloucestershire Archives

APPENDIX B
SOME SIGNIFICANT DATES

1086	Leckhampton included in Domesday Survey
1162	First recorded mention of chapel and priest at Leckhampton
c.1330	Death of Sir John Giffard, built nave, tower and chancel
1340	Bishop of Worcester visits Leckhampton Church
1348-49	Black Death
1539	Dissolution of the monasteries
1541	Leckhampton resubordinated to new Diocese of Gloucester
1649	King Charles beheaded; 1653-58 Cromwell rules as Lord Protector
1660	Charles II restored as King
1670	Date of earliest identifiable gravestone
1688	Five bells cast as a gift of Colonel Henry Norwood
1746	Treble bell added
1827	Lime trees purchased at a cost of 6 shillings
1828	New weathercock fitted, cost of labour 2s 6d
c.1830	Present rectory built
1831-34	Gallery erected over south aisle and vestry added
1840	Original St Philip and St James's church built
1841	School built
1865-66	Church enlarged, porch moved, gallery dismantled
1869	St Philip and St James's becomes independent
1885	Church lit by gas
1886	Deanery of Cheltenham formed, including Leckhampton
1886-1929	Parish administered by sequestrator, appointing curates-in-charge
1893	Lych gate built
1894	Leckhampton estate sold
1897	Parish Hall built
1904	Peal of bells increased to eight
1906	Patronage given to Bishop of Gloucester
1911	First pair of dormer windows installed
1913	New pulpit, new gas radiators fitted
1930	Church wired for electricity
1936	New organ installed
1964	Two new pairs of dormer windows installed
1967	New nave altar added
1972	Tower strengthened, bells re-hung
1978	Church Cottages renovated
1980	New choir stalls built near organ
2003	Incumbent appointed as priest-in-charge

APPENDIX C
THE BELLS

The weights of the bells and their inscriptions are as follows:

BELL	WEIGHT				INSCRIPTION
	Cwts	qtrs	lbs	(kg)	
Treble	3	0	20	(161)	John Taylor & Co Loughborough Leicestershire 1904 To the glory of God and in memory of Isabel Richardson Nov 29th 1899[1]
Second	3	1	7	(168)	(Same as on treble)
Third	3	2	24	(189)	John Taylor Loughborough Recast 1972 Hark to our melody A$\ominus$R^2 1746
Fourth	4	1	26	(227)	Robert Jones Rector Anno Dom 1788[3] Recast 1904
Fifth	4	3	2	(242)	John Taylor Loughborough Recast 1972 God save us all Ralph Crump[4] 1688
Sixth	5	1	22	(277)	John Taylor Loughborough 1972[5]
Seventh	6	3	24	(354)	John Taylor Loughborough Recast 1972 I Rudhall fecit 1833 Canon Eric Brewin Rector James Walford Geoffrey Eveleigh Churchwardens Eric Taylor Belfry Captain
Tenor	9	1	14	(476)	John Taylor Loughborough Recast 1972 Sumptibus Hen Norwood de Leckhampton Recast 1858 C&G Mears

The tenor is the keynote, in A flat, the others being tuned to it in a major scale.

Footnotes:

[1] The date of Isabel Richardson's death.
[2] A rebus for Abel Rudhall
[3] An error for 1688. A plaque in the belfry gives the correct date.
[4] A Ralph Crump had been a churchwarden earlier in the century.
[5] The old sixth, not now in the ring but preserved in Cheltenham Museum, carries the inscription 'wee ware all cast by Abrã Rudhall Glos 1688' with the coat of arms of James II on the waist.

APPENDIX D
SPECIFICATION OF THE ORGAN
Built 1936 by Hill, Norman & Beard, modified 2000

Pedal Organ C -g^1, 32 notes

1. Open Diapason		16
2. Bourdon	(from 9)	16
3. Octave	(extension of 1)	8
4. Bass Flute	(extension of 2)	8
5. Flute	(extension of 2)	4
6. Fifteenth		4
7. Twenty second	(extension of 6)	2
8. Double Trumpet	(from 27)	16

   i. Great to Pedal
   ii. Swell to Pedal
  iii. Choir to Pedal

Swell Organ (enclosed) C - c^4, 61 notes

20. Open Diapason			8
21. Rohr Flöte			8
22. Vox Angelica (c^0)			8
23. Salicional			8
24. Gemshorn			4
25. Fifteenth			2
26. Mixture III	2	$1^1/_3$	1
27. Double Trumpet			16
28. Trumpet	(from 27)		8
29. Oboe			8
30. Clarion	(from 27)		4

     Tremulant
  viii. Octave
   ix. Suboctave
   x. Unison off

Great Organ C - c^4, 61 notes

9. Contra Rohrflöte			16
10. Open Diapason 1			8
11. Open Diapason 2			8
12. Wald Flöte			8
13. Lieblich Gedeckt	(from 31)		8
14. Dulciana	(from 32)		8
15. Principal			4
16. Harmonic Flute	(from 33)		4
17. Fifteenth			2
18. Rauschquint II	(from 35)	$1^1/_3$	1
19. Tromba	(from 36)		8

   iv. Swell to Great
   v. Choir to Great
   vi. Choir Suboctave to Great
  vii. Great & Pedal Pistons coupled

Choir Organ (enclosed) C - c^4, 61 notes

31. Lieblich Gedeckt		8
32. Dulciana		8
33. Harmonic Flute		4
34. Stopped Flute		2
35. Rauschquint II	$1^1/_3$	1
36. Tromba		8
37. Clarinet		8

     Tremulant
   xi. Octave
   xii. Suboctave
  xiii. Unison off
  xiv. Swell to Choir

Balanced expression pedals to Swell & Choir. Electro-pneumatic action incorporating solid-state logic system. Duplex blower by Watkins & Watson.

With acknowledgements to Roy Williamson and John Wright

APPENDIX E
SELECT BIBLIOGRAPHY

Below are listed some of the main sources. If not generally available, a copy of most of them may be found in the Local Studies Department of Cheltenham Public Library (CPL), Gloucester City Library or the Gloucestershire Archives (GA – formerly Gloucestershire Record Office). (*TBGAS*) stands for the *Transactions of the Bristol and Gloucester Archaeological Society.*

GENERAL HISTORIES OF THE COUNTY AND LOCALITY

Sir R Atkyns. *Ancient and Present State of Gloucestershire.* 1712.

R Bigland. *Historical, Monumental and Genealogical Collections relating to the County of Gloucestershire.* 1791 -1889.

T D Fosbroke. *History of the County of Gloucestershire.* 1807.

G Hart. *A History of Cheltenham.* 1965.

A Miles. *History of Cheltenham* (10 volumes, manuscript). (CPL)

S Rudder. *A New History of Gloucestershire.* 1779.

ACCOUNTS OF LECKHAMPTON

G B Witts. *Early History of Leckhampton.* 1884.

R C Barnard. *Records of Leckhampton.* 1897

Leckhampton W I. *The Story of our Village, 1850 -1957.*

Leckhampton W I. *Our Village, then and now.* 1977.

E D Andrew and E W Brewin. *Leckhampton through the Ages.* 1979.

E H Miller. *Leckhampton Yesteryear.* 1996

ARCHITECTURAL AND OTHER STUDIES

W H Bird. *Old Gloucestershire Churches.* 1928.

M Bliss and F Sharpe. *Church Bells of Gloucestershire.* 1986.

M Bliss. *The Last Years of John Rudhall, Bellfounder of Gloucester. TBGAS,* 2003.

R and J A Brandon. *Parish Churches.* 1849.

L W Cowie. *Dictionary of British Social History.* 1973.

C T Davies. *Monumental Brasses of Gloucestershire.* 1899.

J Fendley. *Chancellor Parson's Notes on the Diocese of Gloucester.* 2005.

S Friar. *A Companion to the English Parish Church.* 1966.

S R Glynne. *Gloucestershire Church Notes.* 1902.

A Hartshorne. *Monumental Effigies near Cheltenham.*

I M Roper. *Monumental Effigies of Gloucestershire.* 1931

D Verey and A Brooks. The 'Buildings of England' series – *Gloucestershire, the Vale and the Forest of Dean.* 1970, 2002.

PERIODICALS

Leckhampton Parish Magazines. Various dates, 1888 onwards. (Some in CPL)
Transactions of the Bristol and Gloucester Archaeological Society.
Gloucestershire Notes and Queries, various volumes.
Gloucester (and Bristol) Diocesan Calendar, 1859 onwards. (GA)
The Cheltenham Examiner (CPL)
The Cheltenham Looker-on (CPL)
The Ringing World, August 11, 1972 and (article by D Bagley) 29 July 1994.
Cheltenham Local History Society *Journal* 20 (article by A Munden on 1851 Religious Census).

DOCUMENTARY SOURCES

'Hockaday Abstracts' from diocesan registers, etc. (GA).

Vestry minutes, churchwardens' accounts, specifications, plans, bills, receipts and correspondence (GA), chiefly in the catalogue series P198a and P198/1 but also in VI/144 (Bishop's transcripts, 1601 - 1811), D2970/90 (Middleton's plans), D3867 (the Paterson papers), F1/1/— (Faculties), D5/1/29 and D177 III/8 (re Advowson), D16/3/18(200) (re Sequestration), *inter alia.*

National Archives HO 129/344 (Religious Census)

Ecclesiastical Commissioners' File No 43118 (Church of England Record Centre)

Library of the Council for the Care of Churches

THE REVEREND CHARLES BRANDON TRYE AND HIS SONS

Top left, Canon Charles Brandon Trye. *Top right*, Reginald Trye preaching in an unidentified church and *below* with his family in front of the rectory, *c*. 1890.

Courtesy of Chris Trye and Rex Trye

Henry Norwood Trye II. He was the older son of Canon Charles Brandon Trye and is not to be confused with his uncle of the same name.

An engraving of the church during Canon Charles Brandon Trye's incumbency, by G P Johnson in Norman's *History of Cheltenham*, 1863

FEES PAYABLE
TO THE
MINISTER & PARISH CLERK
OF THE
Parish of Leckhampton.

	MINISTER.			CLERK.		
	£.	s.	d.	£.	s.	d.
Publication of Banns	0	2	0	0	1	0
Marriage by Licence	0	10	6	0	5	0
Marriage by Banns	0	6	0	0	3	0
Churching	0	0	6			
Certificates from Register	0	2	6			
Funerals of Inhabitant Householder (except at three o'clock in winter and four o'clock in summer)	0	10	6	0	5	0
Funeral of Non-Parishioner	2	2	0	1	1	0

FEES PAYABLE TO THE
RECTOR of LECKHAMPTON,
For Vaults, Tombstones, Tablets, &c.

	£.	s.	d.
Vaults in the Church or Chancel	52	10	0
Ditto in the Churchyard	21	0	0
Brick Graves in the Church	21	0	0
Ditto in the Churchyard	8	8	0
Opening a Vault	3	3	0
Head and Footstone	1	1	0
Erecting a Monument or Tablet, if not exceeding six superficial feet	5	5	0
For every additional foot	1	1	0
Flat Stone in the Churchyard	3	3	0
Ditto, with Iron Fence	4	4	0

CHARLES BRANDON TRYE, *Rector.*
1832.

J. J. Hadley, Printer, Journal Office, Cheltenham.

Table of fees contributing to the income of the Rector
and the Parish Clerk in 1832

Two watercolour views of the church painted by unknown artists in about 1800. *Above,* from the collection of the author, *below,* courtesy of Margaret Walford.

Eric Miller is Chairman of the Leckhampton Local History Society and its Co-ordinator of Research. Since his retirement from the Civil Service he has spent much of his time researching the history of Cheltenham and its environs. He has written books on the history of Leckhampton Court (*Manor House to Hospice*), on aspects of village life in Leckhampton (*Leckhampton Yesteryear*) and, together with other members of the Society, on Leckhampton in the Second World War. In 2000, together with Alan Gill, he edited '*Britain in Old Photographs – Leckhampton*', which gained them an award from the Cheltenham Arts Council. He has also had articles on local history printed in a number of periodicals, including the journal of the British Association for Local History.

He first came to live in Leckhampton in 1959 and since 1969 he and his family have been closely involved with activities at St Peter's. He has served on the Parochial Church Council and was its Honorary Secretary from 1978 to 1981.